DATE DUE

Great African Americans

ZORA NEALE HURSTON

Writer and Storyteller

Revised Edition

Patricia and Fredrick McKissack

Series Consultant
Dr. Russell L. Adams, Chairman
Department of Afro-American Studies, Howard University

Enslow Publishers, Inc.

40 Industrial Road	PO Box 38
Box 398	Aldershot
Berkeley Heights, NJ 07922	Hants GU12 6BP
USA	UK

http://www.enslow.com

To Neysa, Martha, Carol, Joyce, and Ellen: Wow!

Copyright © 2002 by Enslow Publishers, Inc.

Revised edition of *Zora Neale Hurston: Writer and Storyteller* © 1992

Library of Congress Cataloging-in-Publication Data

McKissack, Pat, 1944–
    Zora Neale Hurston, writer and storyteller / Patricia and Fredrick McKissack.— Rev. ed.
      p. cm. — (Great African Americans)
    Includes index.
    ISBN 0-7660-1694-3
    1. Hurston, Zora Neale—Juvenile literature. 2. Authors, American—20th century—Biography—Juvenile
literature. 3. Folklorists—United States—Biography—Juvenile literature. 4. African American women
authors—Biography—Juvenile literature. [1. Hurston, Zora Neale. 2. Authors, American. 3. African
Americans—Biography. 4. Women—Biography.] I. McKissack, Fredrick. II. Title.
    PS3515.U789 Z784 2001
    813'.52—dc21
                        00–013085

To Our Readers: We have done our best to make sure all Internet Addresses in this book were active and appropriate when we went to press. However, the author and the publisher have no control over and assume no liability for the material available on those Internet sites or on other Web sites they may link to. Any comments or suggestions can be sent by e-mail to comments@enslow.com or to the address on the back cover.

Every effort has been made to locate all copyright holders of material used in this book. If any errors or omissions have occurred, corrections will be made in future editions of this book.

Illustration Credits: Beinecke Rare Book and Manuscript Library, Yale University, pp. 4, 16, 17, 30; Courtesy of Wellesley College Archives, p. 26; Department of Special Collections, George A. Smathers Libraries, University of Florida, pp. 9, 11, 24; Kurt Weber, Enslow Publishers, Inc., p. 10; Library of Congress, pp. 6, 7, 15, 19, 20, 23, 27; Photo by Carl Van Vechten, used with permission of the Van Vechten Trust, print from Beinecke Rare Book and Manuscript Library Collection, p. 21; Photo from the Langston Hughes Collection at the Yale Beinecke Library published by permission of Harold Ober Associates, Inc., p. 14; Photographs and Prints Division, Schomburg Center for Research in Black Culture, The New York Public Library, Astor, Lenox and Tilden Foundations, p. 3; Print courtesy Stetson Kennedy Collection, University of Florida Library, pp. 13, 25; Yale Collection of American Literature, Beinecke Rare Book and Manuscript Library, 1937, p. 29.

Cover Credits: Library of Congress

TABLE of CONTENTS

Zora Neale Hurston
January 7, 1891–January 28, 1960

CHAPTER 1

"Jump at the Sun"

Zora was born in 1891 about five miles from Orlando, Florida, in a small town named Eatonville. It was an all-black town founded in 1886.

Zora's father, John Hurston, was a preacher. She and her father didn't get along well. He often spanked Zora for being "sassy."

But her mother, Lucy Hurston, made Zora her special child. Lucy told her daughter to "jump at the sun." Zora grew up jumping, running, and playing

"Jump at the sun!" As a child, Zora loved outdoor games. As a grown-up, above left, she still liked to play.

in the Florida sunshine. Zora was tough. She knew how to fight, so the boys let her play with them. But the young girl also loved learning about things. She would slip under the porch to read. Her mother made sure Zora had plenty to read.

6

Zora always liked going to Joe Clarke's store in Eatonville. Men and women sat on the porch and told stories. Zora enjoyed the stories her neighbors told about tricky rabbits and strong black men. They called these stories "big 'ol lies."

When Zora was thirteen years old, her mother died. Her father married again right away. Zora didn't like her stepmother. And she still did not get along with her father.

Soon Zora was old enough to understand her mother's words. It was time to "jump at the sun!" She couldn't really jump high enough to touch the sun. But if she tried, at least she would be up off the ground. As soon as she could, Zora left home.

Zora listened when the adults gathered to talk on the porch of a general store like this.

7

CHAPTER 2

On the Road

Zora joined a traveling show company. She took care of the costumes. She spent long hours mending and sewing, packing and unpacking. It was hard work. But at least she was away from the father and stepmother she didn't like. Zora felt lucky that she was getting to see some of the world.

Still, she never gave up the idea of going back to school. In 1917 Zora left the show company. She went to a high school in Baltimore, Maryland.

**Zora did
not get
along
with her
stepmother,
so she
left home.**

She had one dress, one pair of shoes, and no money. She graduated from high school in June 1918.

Then she went to college in Washington, D.C., for two years. During that time, Zora began writing. She was asked to join a writers' group at the college. Zora wrote her first short story, "John Redding Goes to Sea." It was printed in the writers' group magazine, *The Stylus*, in May 1921. Zora knew then that she could be a writer.

Zora helped with costumes for a traveling show.

Zora, center, with classmates at Howard University in Washington, D.C. Zora began writing in college.

CHAPTER 3

Making It in New York

In the 1920s many African Americans were leaving the South and moving to northern cities. Many of them moved to New York City. Zora went there in 1925.

She settled in Harlem, a mostly black neighborhood in New York City. In the 1920s, many African-American writers, artists, and musicians lived and worked there. Their work was fresh and different. This famous period of time

Zora's writing was different. She wrote about southern blacks and used the language she heard them speak.

was called the Harlem Renaissance. Zora Neale Hurston was one of those fresh young writers.

Zora, with writers Langston Hughes, center, and Jessie Fauset, left. The statue honors Booker T. Washington.

A lot of white people were interested in Harlem. Many of them wanted to help the young writers, too. They met the writers and poets at parties and helped them get their work into magazines and books. These people were called patrons.

Harlem was an exciting place to live. People found many ways to have fun.

One person who helped Zora was Mrs. Charlotte Osgood Mason. She was a very, very rich woman who was a patron to Zora and several other writers and artists.

Zora entered a writing contest. Two of her short stories won. So she was invited to the awards dinner. Fannie Hurst, a white writer, was a judge in the contest. She liked Zora's work very much. They met at the awards dinner. Hurst learned that Zora needed a job so she could go back to college. She hired Zora to be her secretary.

At last Zora had enough money to go back to school. Up until that time, she had worked two or three jobs to make ends meet.

Charlotte Mason liked Zora's work and wanted her to write more.

Hurst also helped Zora get into Barnard College, a women's college at

16

Columbia University in New York City. Zora was the only black woman at Barnard at the time.

During that time Zora still wrote stories. And her writing was getting stronger and better. She graduated from Barnard in 1928.

At Barnard College in New York City, Zora began to study African-American folklore.

CHAPTER 4

The Voice of Her People

Z ora was very interested in studying the ways different people lived. She listened to their stories and folklore. With the help of her patrons, Zora traveled all over the South gathering African-American stories. Her research was like sitting on Joe Clarke's store porch listening to people tell stories all the time. She loved it!

Zora was one of the first African Americans to

**Zora learned about different kinds of worship.
Here she beats a drum used in some ceremonies.**

write these stories down. These were the stories of her people, and she recorded them in the language of her people. She would write about a storm like this: "God was grumbling his thunder and playing the zigzag lighting thru his fingers."

Her book *Mules and Men* was a collection of her stories. It was written in 1935. Zora was well known for her short stories. In the 1930s she also wrote three novels. The most famous of them was *Their Eyes Were Watching God*, written in 1937. She also wrote her life story, *Dust Tracks on a Road*, in 1942.

Zora, left, traveled through the South to hear people's stories and songs.

**Zora also wrote scripts for a radio station in Ohio
and helped write some plays.**

CHAPTER 5

A Very Special Writer

People enjoyed being around Zora. She charmed them with stories about her life in Eatonville. Sometimes her stories were true. Sometimes they weren't. Very few people ever knew the difference.

Zora was married twice, but not for long. She didn't talk about that much. Her first love was writing and her second was her freedom.

Zora continued to study and write about

folklore during the 1930s and 1940s. She traveled through the South, and to Central America, South America, Haiti, and Jamaica. There, she gathered the stories people told.

People liked Zora. She was happy and always the life of the party.

In 1948 Zora was falsely accused of hurting a child. She was arrested, but it was all a mistake. She had been in Central America at the time of the crime. The charges were dropped, but she was very upset.

By now, all the parties were over. All the friends had gone. Zora chose to live alone in the South, away from friends and family. But she didn't feel sorry for herself.

Zora didn't write much in

Zora, center, believed every person had a story to tell, and she was always ready to listen.

her last years, except for a few articles and short stories. Her books didn't make a lot of money. When she ran out of money, she would take a job as a maid.

She moved back to New York in 1957 to work

Zora, front, went to Jamaica, Haiti, and South America to learn about the local folklore.

on a book. The book was never finished. Zora moved back to Florida and died a poor woman on January 28, 1960. She was buried in an unmarked grave.

Zora Neale Hurston might have been forgotten if it hadn't been for Alice Walker, another black writer. She worked hard to have Zora's old stories turned into books again. Walker had a headstone placed on Zora's grave in 1973.

Thanks to writer Alice Walker, above, Zora's books became popular once again.

Zora wrote the stories people told her. They were a lot like the stories she heard when she was growing up. If she hadn't gathered them, those stories might have been lost forever.

Zora's stories are special because she knew how to write in the language of real people.

1891 ~ Born January 7 in Eatonville, Florida.

1921 ~ Publishes first story, "John Redding Goes to Sea."

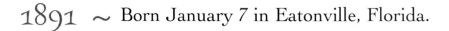

1925 ~ Moves to New York City. Enters Barnard College.

1927 ~ Goes to Florida to gather folklore stories.

1928 ~ Graduates from Barnard College.

1934 ~ Publishes first novel, *Johah's Gourd Vine*.

1935 ~ Publishes *Mules and Men*, a folklore collection. Travels to Jamaica and Haiti to learn their folklore.

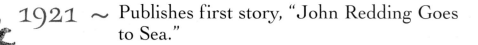

1937 ~ Publishes novel *Their Eyes Were Watching God*.

1942 ~ Publishes *Dust Tracks on a Road*, the story of her life.

1960 ~ Dies on January 28 in Fort Pierce, Florida.

WORDS TO KNOW

folklore—Customs, beliefs, and stories that were not written down, but are passed by word of mouth from one generation to another.

graduate—To finish the required studies at a school.

Harlem—A mostly black neighborhood in New York City.

Harlem Renaissance—During the 1920s, young black writers, artists, and musicians began showing the black experience in a bold new way. They spoke about being proud, beautiful people. Renaissance means "an awakening" or "rebirth."

Their Eyes Were Watching God is Zora's novel about a young black woman.

novel—A fictional story that is long enough to fill a whole book.

patron—Someone, often a very rich person, who gives money and other help to artists or writers so they can do their work. Zora was able to go to school, travel, and write because she had several patrons.

research—To gather information for study or for discovery.

secretary—A person who manages the day-to-day work of an office or assists others with their work. Fannie Hurst hired Zora as her secretary.

short story—A short piece of fiction, often published in newspapers and magazines.

traveling show company—A group of performers who travel from place to place, putting on shows.

Zora researched the stories of African Americans.

Learn more about Zora Neale Hurston

Books

Calvert, Roz. *Zora Neale Hurston: Storyteller of the South*.
    Broomall, Penn.: Chelsea House Publishers, 1993.

Miller, William. *Zora Hurston and the Chinaberry Tree*.
    New York: Lee & Low Books, Inc., 1996.

Porter, A. P. *Jump at de Sun: The Story of Zora Neale Hurston*.
    Minneapolis, Minn.: Lerner Publishing Group, 1992.

Internet Addresses

Voices from the Gaps: Women Writers of Color
Biography, related links
    <http://voices.cla.umn.edu/vg/>

National Women's Hall of Fame: Zora Neale Hurston
Short biography
    <http://www.greatwomen.org/women.
        php?action=viewone&id=83>

i.am/zora: Zora Neale Hurston
Biography, photographs, essays, related links
    <http://pages.prodigy.com/zora/content.htm>

index